# Color Advisory Board

Published by Gunpowder Press
Edited by David Starkey and Chryss Yost
PO Box 60035
Santa Barbara, CA 93160-0035

Front cover: Illustration from *Zur Farbenlehre ("Theory of Colors")*
by Johann Wolfgang von Goethe (1810).

ISBN-13: 978-1-957062-26-6

Library of Congress Control Number: 2026905866

www.gunpowderpress.com

Gunpowder Press is part of Gunpowder Poetry, a 501(c)(3) nonprofit
literary organization. The Barry Spacks Poetry Prize is supported in
part by the Santa Barbara Poetry Fund under the auspices of the Santa
Barbara Foundation.

# Color Advisory Board

Poems

## Michele Santamaría

Gunpowder Press • Santa Barbara
2026

*ain't cut drylongsoher/songs so many-hued/
hum some blues in technicolor/pick a violet guitar*

*—Harryette Mullen*

*They say that beauty is in the eye of the beholder and that ugly is as
ugly does. Both are lies. Ugly is everything done to you in the name
of beauty. Knowing the difference is part of getting free.*

*—Tressie McMillan Cottom*

# Contents

Invocation

May red intoxicate with its grasp,
may green satisfy the fingertips' gaze,
may blue soothe what cannot be calmed,

until my four year old draws my coral
cardigan across burnished shoulders,
more grace than Grace Jones

or Grace Kelly when he steps into jade
ocean, half blurred & unsteadied,
human & prismatic expanse.

COCA COLA RED

Red Laments

Was I the broken or breaking thing,
A seethe of molten rock, slow scald

Against the mountainside, peeling
Back flesh from bone, ruby-raw?

The maw, with swollen gum, mother-
Daughter telltale jaw, the flowering

Mark before the bruise, the rouge
& lips perched around a cigarette—

I'd give anything to touch those lips,
To touch that stain & stain the world

With my permanence. People feel safe
Clutching other colors while holding me

In their marrow. It is one thing to be
Chosen and another to be undeniable,

The color that oozes from the surface
After the deepest incision.

## Simultaneous Translation

*Gehen, gehen, gehen*: to go and go and go, to pack and relocate,
*desempacar*. The word she says to make them laugh: *Sicherheits-*

*überprufung*, airport security, and then there's *Schlag*, an unpleasant sound
but not taste whipped rich over cake. Her relatives in Vienna, how they
said, *te pareces a tu mamá*.

No one had ever said that. Hunger. *Hungrig*. Scurrying like a rat. Not
like *quiero*.

I—

want, love? *Wohin, woher*—there; I always got confused between *allá* and
*aquí* and *el*, not feminine, *azúcar*, sugar beneath the tongue.

Verbs—I remember—prefer, like the blurred tadpoles at my feet. Small
*piedras*, beneath, they seemed to cut less than rocks. Cradle, *cuna* emptied
into soft brown arms.

Cold

water: my rolled pants in the river, *mis pantalones mojados*. *Erster Wort*:
Father. *Kindern, kinder*. *Papá*. *Te espero en el agua*.

Here,

*aquí, papá*. Listen, it's like my blood's ebb and flow, *en mis venas, en mis
ríos*. *Papá*. Tremulous. *Tremendo, el miedo*, this fear, day and night.

In the envelope of my body, I've kept the question that will not die:

*liebchen*, how could you leave us?  I have no other recourse but to ask.
*Recuerda, recuerdo*, forget, remember.

Almost

a record, a drawing I sent her.  *Cuadro, cuarto*: white room where our
family waits.
The same drawing sent twice.  *Madre*, daughter cradled in her arms.
Mother, *Mutter*:

we both felt abandoned.  The tide that will come and go, leaving a trail of
demands: *vergessen, bitte*.  Forget.  *Olvida*.  Pack the black suitcase, *hija*.

Drive.

In Search of Rita Hayworth

> *In 1946, an expedition into the wilderness of Canada's unexplored Headless
> Valley came across an abandoned trapper's shack. In it the expedition found
> three things: a candle, a can of beans, and a picture of Rita.*

I find her in my mother's face
speaking to a waiter, a woman
wanting to be wanted

and succeeding by his glance,

the bewilderment of that
like stepping into the blinding
sunlight of a Tijuana afternoon

after waking up.  Not the sun

a young woman sees after being
raped by her father in the morning
and then being expected to dance

away the afternoons by his side.

Before the studio raised her hairline,
before Hayworth perfected a glance,
Margarita Cansino learned how

to dance from the man who may

or may not have raped her
and later we see her beam as she
dances by Fred Astaire's side,

as she becomes a gypsy, or a cover

girl, or possibly a likeness glued onto
an A-bomb dropped in a Pacific atoll,
whose impossibly turquoise waters

beckon like the embodiment of some

goddess and not the bones we might
find if we went to Holy Cross Cemetery,
Culver City, California, USA

in the Grotto section, L196, #6.

Technicolor Sonnet

Just to be longing, belong to it,
the color created through prismatic
beams, light, so much light that the denizens
of Oz lost gallons of water from the heat,
lights burning for saturated color,
an ideal, an idea, an id amok
on set, tearing through costumes, yelling
more light, more light, or as Batty says
in *Blade Runner*: "more life, I want more life"
I want my reds redder than red, ruby
slippers to take me back to ground zero,
apocalyptic wheat fields, me, naked,
umbilical cord unwrapped from my neck,
a new mythology for me, more life.

My Mother claims that we are related to Hedy Lamarr

On a good day, my mother resembles Mariska Hargitay, which makes her Pop Rocks, kohl eyeliner, all froth and buzz. Any woman who resembles my mother is unsettling. It could be anyone. An actress, a bus driver, a nun. Moreover, how long will any pop culture reference last? Hedy Lamarr, aka Hedwig Eva Maria Kiesler, has the right kind of cultural capital, those ruby red lips with that classic cola aftertaste, that ritzy font. Hedy Lamarr, she of *Samson and Delilah* fame, she of Technicolor dreams and one of our ancestors, a progenitor according to my mom. That Austro-Hungarian Viennese gal with the leggy legs who went to Hollywood and who made time to hobnob with the eggheads. And, yes, that gal, an inventor who had it in her to make bombs smart. Ah, poor Hedy, though it's such a cliché, they were always looking at your boobs while you waxed technological. Smart bombs. They think they know so much. Today, I'm feeling smug, feeling like Delilah, plucking, gnashing, throwing ruby orbs called grapes as I watch Samson tear down the temple. Poor Samson. So powerful. So impotent. So, so and then again. Then again, I do my best, try my best to not be related to anyone and to believe that all there ever was, was my mother and father in some post-apocalyptic version of Eden, clinging to one another, the last survivors, the last survivors of a crash, an airplane floating in an ocean and me watching their legs treading water from below. Me, a great white shark.

Run, Hide, Fight

I'd like to think
I'd follow best advice,
To run, or crawl beneath,
Or if need be, claw
The jugular—instead,
I often think
I'd freeze
Hopefully not throw
Someone else
In front of me—
Who likes to weigh
If they would do
The worst thing
Possible, except
Consider this—
To what degree
Are you alive
Because someone
Decided to be
Selfish, not just run
But throw somebody else
Down from the walls
While screaming
*Not me, not me, not me.*

Today I Met Pandemic Barbie

So I put on my red lipstick
because red is the perfect color
for Zoom and for Technicolor,

& my nemesis looked tired,
having recently given birth.
Still, that Madonna-&-Child smugness

in the glaze of her indecisively-
colored eyes—not green, not hazel,
camouflage of grey cashmere, no pilling—

ponytail signaling the right angle,
tight angles of womanhood as well
as optimism because Cheerful,

because Womanhood is white,
holding its white infant close
to its bosom & to think I could have

contemplated winning this round by staging
more put-together, more polished,
when everything about the way I look

is wrong, so she could slum it
in a T-shirt because white womanhood
is expensive even when it's slumming

in a T-shirt & especially when it's crying
crocodile as it conjures a black boy whistling
& trying to grab it with his hands.

Technicolor Sonnet

More alive, a new mythology for me:
to be the kind of gal who's froth over
black coffee, a tilted hat, thinly arched
eyebrows, light footsteps, hand resting on
an arm as if to reassure, insure
some debt; what is love if not debt, a pound
of flesh, oh my daughter, oh my ducats,
my mother might have said and nothing
I can or have ever done would erase
the debt, the account book always red,
to dream of a red redder than red,
what could be so bad as that, to want
and want, to rearrange the actors again?

I'm Having My Carmen Miranda Moment

Heck, I got the cha-cha tatas,
I've got the baba running down
my chin, I've got a star-spangled
rope tied around my thigh &
I'm still dancing away boys,
The Gang's All Here, set to watch me
swivel my hips red, to raw &
jiggle, to readjust my lemon, banana, apple
Dole United Fruit Company headdress,
Hey—the gang's all here, anchors
aweigh, with my heart racing, racing, racing
must have been one too many pills, one too many
colors in my costume, yellow has become
too heavy, & I've got to fall on my knees, burn
with the blaze of a tacky tachycardic event—
it's okay my honeys, as long as you keep
stroking my cheek with your gaze,
what else can ease the gaping loneliness
except the boundless love of the stage
until the weight of it all pulls you down
beneath the waves, Yemaya's hands around
your ankles and an anchor tied around your waist,
heart beating a Kentucky Derby—Anchors aweigh,
my boys. Anchors aweigh.

Rin Tin Tin dies in my mother's, not Jean Harlow's, arms

Rin Tin Tin senior, Rin Tin Tin the progenitor, Rin Tin Tin the first sired, in his munificence, 48 puppies, some bequeathed to Hollywood royalty like Greta Garbo and Jean Harlow and that's how it came to be, that some permutation of Rin Tin Tin died in Jean Harlow's arms. My mother claimed that her father had a dog just like Rin Tin Tin.  In my mother's scrapbooks, there are childhood vacations, black and white photographs, no postcards, there is the intelligent profile of a blurred dog and my mother's face out of focus though I could tell that she was happy, her happiness even then as a child was willful, splendid, I'd think as unlikely an event as it would have been throughout her life since my mother has always been consistent in her inconsistencies.  If she had had a German Shepherd whom she cherished, he must have been as good as Rinty.  Maybe she rode his sable haunches into combat.  My mother was made for battle, for leading armies, not for breastfeeding, scraping dishes, spilling soda, not for watching me conduct an autopsy on her grilled chicken. My mother was meant for Technicolor visions, for riding into battle flanked by Joan of Arc and Marlon Brando, James Dean and Madame Curie, a cast of thousands thronging while she radiated beatific certainty. My mother would not have smiled, would not have beamed, would not have loved if her dog had not been, most faithfully, worthy of a sepulchre in *Le Cimetière des Chiens*.

BLUE VELVET

Girl as the Color Feral

Girl with hair in her face.
Girl with dirt on her palms.
Girl who has an avenger,
Light caught on her walls;
Sometimes a wolf,

Sometimes an angel,
Friend and foe to prayers
That slip from her lips while
Bloodied Christs writhe, impaled
Insects inside golden church domes,

Barnacled gold and green is her
Birthplace, with its mountains,
Its beggars lodged in her throat,
Not anything much
Like the isthmus where she lives

Ocean days and picks up white shells
One by one, skipping past distended
Cobalt balloons, man-o-wars trembling
Skin aroused. Two bodies together,
Blistered red, sand-wet in a fade
Of heat, that smear across the lens.

Girl watching the sun pulse orange,
Collapse into purple and then fade darker,
The bluish-black she knows most resembles
Her innards which she could get to
With her muzzle, blood-red, raw.

# To be Rita Hayworthed, First Variation

Misery clings, a dress after downpour
sinks deeper into flesh until you can't tell
the difference between your flesh and its skin,
slinks through your dreams, all cinema siren,
waits for you to chase her & when you awake
cotton-mouthed, stunned
Misery is no longer Gilda, aka Rita Hayworth.
It's sad, sad, Margarita Cansino
who danced every afternoon
of her youth with the man who likely raped her.
Her father, so elegant in his flamenco,
so elegant in the way he trained her
not to wince when Hollywood raised her hairline,
so elegant as his pasodoble turned and turned,
the tacón of his shoe, you see—that *rat-ta-tap* heel
grinding the floor & her—outstretched,
forever available in film
to the appraisal of strangers. Little girl.

Slut

My bathing suit was Coca Cola red as the thin stream
of blood started flowing, my body model lean & supple
as an otter in the water, boys teasing me—
splashing, swimming round—as though we were all
an unlikely bevy of creatures—quite unlike the body
I grew into by thirteen, bombshell pin-up, peach
bandeau top under a white linen jacket until the rumors
began. *Maybe worst of all worst of all worst
of all, maybe she likes it.* I started to wear my father's
suits, bespoke for him, too boxy for my figure—asked for
a foot of my raven hair to be cut off and I walked
around sad as a woman who's just found out her sister
was her husband's latest conquest. La Llorona, all that
splendid raven hair in tufts around her chair, the scissors
sharp against her forehead as though a threat or perhaps
some kind of promise. *Do not betray me, love.  Do not
betray me. The woods are full of bodies. My steps are light.*

Color Advisory Service, Second Variation

In 1952, Natalie Kalmus gave
her name to a black and white
TV console after devoting her life
to Technicolor, or rather, serving
as head of the Color Advisory Service,

which was not in charge of deciding
that my nose was too broad for someone
half Eastern European, which was not an agency
for determining the proper degrees
of miscegenation for making pretty

über-model babies, which was instead
the department which oversaw each
minor detail in a Technicolor movie,
like how red the actors' noses might
get because of the wind and how

displeasing red would have been,
or how many munchkins would get
to wear red if it were offset
by white which would be offset by
the green and the blue of the sky

because Natalie Kalmus, before giving
her name to a brand of TV was devoured
by her need to practice color-restraint
to imitate nature when she could have
feasted on color. Instead, she made charts

for each movie she supervised, stayed
divorced from her husband for twenty odd
years before telling anyone, fell for the lies
of some psychic she met in Las Vegas
& left her papers to the Oscar's Library

where I learn little else except that someone
aside from her husband still loved her
and that she kept his note asking for lunch
*For old time's sake*, that she wrote a short
story set in Hawaii, that maybe was meant

to be a movie, and that someone called Bob
got stuck in Rio while filming a picture.
I expected her to be more powerful than this
as if she could outwit the desperate need
to be found beautiful. There it was in her story

how the main female character wanted so badly
to be seen, to be made known through beauty.
Oh Natalie—why not be ugly? Why not make
the colors rain down upon the set, in torrents
that no eye alive or dead could forget?

## Estée Lauder Beauty Counter Photograph


*Taken by the Makeover Esthetician*
*Miami, Florida, The Falls Mall, 1986*

Every which way I look, this face is wrong—
from the crooked bulb of her nose
to the way her neck is short, strong,

a stump beneath round face & ears long
in proportion to her chin; hands, & toes
too elegant in comparison, just wrong;

especially her nose, nose, let's go along
& brush the bridge to minimize this nose,
like her neck—too thick, too strong,

when it should be slender—wrong
in all the ways I can't fix. Growing
up looking like this should make her long

for what I can do to make it gone,
or at the very least, minimize: that nose,
that neck too stocky, short, & strong—

how can makeup be enough to fix these wrongs?
Should we fix her face & break her nose?
If we believe the camera, let's make it gone.
Everything about her face is wrong.

Brown Villanelle

Fingernails, palms, shapes of hands, ears, teeth—
what is beauty if not a constant test?
Who gets to glide through life, between

sororities & churches, forego genealogy,
instead pass the Brown Paper Bag Test.
Fingernails, palms, shapes of hands, ears, teeth—

are all these scrutinized or just the gleaming
face? Light copper (better), high yellow (best)
for getting to glide through life between

one echelon & the next, aiming to bequeath
something more secure to the next
set of fingernails, palms, shape of hands, ears, teeth—

some firmer grasp, no need for receipts
or documents, no need to hold one's breath,
to glide through life without the in-between.

*Test, test, test, test, test, test*—death
always slouched against the threshold, skin text
of fingernails, palms, shapes of hands, ears, teeth
clawing for breath between the paper seams.

## The Ballad of the Quito Tenis

Not that my father would ever tell me,
not the man who instructs the driver
to look for someone white like him
when he sends an employee to pick me up

at a hotel lobby and, in a way, he's right.
We don't live the ways of the Quechua;
we don't know for a fact that we're Black,
though the first thing his father-in-law said

upon seeing him was *Schwartze*. The way
other Quiteños say I look *mona* or coastal,
another way to say *black, black, black*.
So what does it mean that my mother told me

that she, Chilean white woman, received
an invitation on heavy cream stock
to the Quito Tenis, and that my father—professor,
*economista*—would never be good enough?

What does it mean to be a woman in a country
that speaks your language, that covets and spits
upon your whiteness. *You think you're so much
better than we are. So do we.*

To be Rita Hayworthed, Second Variation

To be
Properly
Rita Hayworthed, I'd need to have
My hairline raised (never did I consider this
An ethnic giveaway) & my hair dyed anything
But jet black.  Consider "golden brown" or
Auburn, not blonde ambition though to be
Rita Hayworthed would be to aspire towards
Aphrodite-status-sexual napalm. I'd have to diet,
As she did. Once, unbelievably a chubby teenager,
Margarita Casino made a big show of the rituals
That would transform her into Rita—dieting, tennis
& horse riding lessons, not the opportunity to learn
How to sing, which rankled.  Her dancing, yes—
After she could prove herself to play Spanish in *Blood
And Sand* instead of being Spanish—a bit like Julie Andrews
In *Victor/Victoria* playing a woman playing a man playing a woman—
Her body, yes.  Always her body offered up on a plate, the shot
In the negligee which made Orson Welles jot her down as his next
Acquisition until he found that he might be able to pretend
To bed Gilda, would have to wake up with sad, sad, Hayworth—
All her insecurities, doubts. A Jewish woman sang "Put the Blame on Mame"
In *Gilda* while Rita lip-synched & writhed. To be honest, it looked like pain
To me rather than seduction, like she was stripping the long gloves off
Her arms as though stepping out of her own skin, free from all contingencies,
Free to be energy, particles of dust in light.

## Girl as the Color Ugly

Oh Natalie, you would not have approved
of that riot of colors applied to my face,
a bird of paradise with green & orange,
would most likely have approved
the makeup artist's attempts to shade
my nose in such a way as to render it smaller.
The inability to do this well in color film
sank careers—some features too broad
for the new technology, some able to maximize
Technicolor's effects by dying their hair flaming red
or to have the right (always white) complexion.
My mother had taken me to the Estée Lauder counter
to partake in the kind of feminine rite of passage
she could withstand because she would always win—
slender nose, slender lips, eyes rimmed several times over
in kohl, in the portrait on the wall, like a Cleopatra we'd never know.

# Technicolor Sonnet

To rearrange the actors again and want
life to imitate art, to want my mother
to stop batting her eyelashes and lying
upon the train tracks.  To want the truth
and not some family folklore, not some
mythos where, when asked if there were any
relatives left in Vienna, my mother said
*none*, when prodded, *your grandfather got out,*
*Tante Didi, Wolfie, Ruth survived.*
Everyone else died. There are no records
accessible from here, no letters, no marks
of faith.  Only the name Fürst, identified
as Jewish as soon as it slips from my lips,
only what the absence chooses to speak.

# Car Accident, 1978, My Father's Face

Shards of glass fall upon the asphalt
while his face is slit from top to bottom.


He didn't wear a seatbelt. It would have been
dramatic enough to film—his body hurtling


through the windshield & then


72 stitches where a hand could travel from
his temple, down his cheek, stitches


where a hand might mark a gentleness,
stitches without anesthesia or so he said—


my hands steady enough to write this.
Eventually, all bleeding stops.

# Bodies of Proof

**1.**

In the gilded etching, the tree-lined avenue recedes into a brush of pine: a gift from family friends, now estranged, perhaps a blur of pencil in mother's address book. The etching displays Hamburg, a city where my father often did business. My father, the man my mother's father called *schwartze*. Any Jew, Sephardic or Ashkenazi, understands the depth of that insult, more and less than *black*, a hatred greater than disgust. My grandfather, the same man who held my small face between his hands and called me *liebchen*, oh littlest of beloveds, while we walked the streets of Chile.

**2.**

A gringa lying on the street. Her tendons, joints, her hair outstretched behind her. Her blood cleaned off, except around her neck: an imagined trace of Aztec purple (the photo's black and white). The suicide could have shared Diego Rivera's bed; in the same New York exhibit, there is a picture of her standing next to Frida, the wife who'd already been betrayed. The blonde woman smiles. In this photograph, she is not regal. Decades later in a Manhattan gallery, I walk from one photo to another, unsure of where my eyes should settle.

**3.**

My husband comparing food displays, unable to distinguish between chocolate and bean paste the same color. How he loved visiting the temple deer at Nara, watching the animals watch others. Once, I walked a few steps beyond my door and saw a deer up close. It was so real it came across as fake, the way an affectionate stranger bewilders. There was an Ecuadorian girl I once saw, standing on her roof as if awaiting any and all trains. Tan vellum stretched over bone, perhaps an Indian nose. She waved goodbye again and again and never moved.

Prayer

Note octagonal windows native to this region,
The peeling sage and daffodil, the broken tile.

Note the variety of wind chimes: magenta, green
And purple.  In cathedrals, blue stood for Mary;

Colors assigned for the faithful and illiterate to worship.
For months, a couch in front of an abandoned house

Has collected rain in its lap.  While I dip two fingers
In the water, something brushes against my pants.

The Siamese and I have met several times.  At night,
We're the only ones outside and watch windows light up,

Watch leaves float by.  I find myself back home;
The cat follows me to the door, expecting to be let in.

Tonight, it won't give up.  I lift my foot, then stop.
The cat purrs, weaving between my legs, pushing

Its head against my knee repeatedly:
*I am lonely. I am lonely.  I am only one thing.*

## Portrait of Girls as Technicolor

She was the only girl I knew who made it
To Hollywood. A picture of us, arms around
Each other, my tan skin near her pale freckles,
Her hair Peruvian coastal mixed with Italian

Or something else—a reddish blond afro
Unmistakable when I saw her on TV.
We & the rest of her sisters played through
Summers of girlhood, summers of chlorine

& tangled beach hair, Coca Cola red swimsuits.
A different photo shows all of five of us posing
On a fake waterfall & what I see now is only beauty:
My long legs outstretched as seduction & parody,

A slight girl's belly stretching against purple,
Blue, green stripes and my hand waving
To an appreciative audience, to our public.

It was in our faces: how we believed
The world loved us. How we believed
In our beauty without having to speak of it,
Perhaps because Florida was our mother
Who indulged us in color: color of sunsets

(Purple, magenta, yellow); color of sea
(Green & aquamarine); color of breath:
Azure, azure. Azúcar. *Go to bed.*

Ode to Blue

For the sake of love, I will feed you lies,
answer, when pressed, that this ocean's murky jade
is enough when I've known & loved blue

incomparable, turquoise waves twisting
themselves into emerald & then back again
& against the whitest of sand, me walking

hand in hand with my father, stopping to collect
shells from the tides & the sun stinging skin,
skin-stinging sand mixed with water & salt—

the kind of blue that flames inside for the rest
of your life, the way I'd imagine was the case
for Jacques Majorelle when he saw Berber blue

in Marrakech, that blue he had to master,
to fully encapsulate himself
in its molten lapis lazuli.

To say that he invented the pigment
would be a lie, but when have we let lies
stop us from coloring the world we'd like?

Oh, my beloved, your eyes are a cold
blue field, focused elsewhere most of the time
& that is why I can touch you & be touched,

as though we are always in two kayaks
while the blue-tipped wings of a young heron

beat past. So awkwardly elegant, so little

blue, so much grey, so why call them great blue herons?
I don't want to know why. My son's *whys* exhaust me.
I'd rather think of that blue fringe of feathers,

of the blue heron's eyes, of how so much
that is alive thrashes against explanations
& how I would happily wrap myself

in Majorelle blue & drink—no, chew—
big hunks of its freshness, if it would mean
that I could close my eyes & step into that

childhood ocean, green twisting back into
turquoise & then back again to become
an iridescent cobalt.

EMERALD CITY

## Ekphrastic Towards a Family

How to account for my grandmother's eyes
in that portrait, the surprising sharpness

of irises in crayon, not the Technicolor green
I had hoped for, instead, an in-between color

I remember as silver, an unrepentant goddess
unlikely to fulfill the promise that accompanied

the drawing—to come back for her daughter, a pact
my mother only tells me about in this moment,

as she asks me if I remember where I last saw
the portrait, after asking if I remember it,

& I try to think only of another drawing
in my mother's house—a reproduction of a Picasso—

the baby's hand clasping the mother's cheek
while the mother grasps whatever she can.

Technicolor Green

1.
What is known: that you walked past
Chilean immigration unimpeded, wearing
24 karat gold bracelets, declaring them *de*

*fantasía*, no—not real, in your adopted tongue.
I would add that you laughed as you took
hold of grandfather's arm, a coquette's laugh,

not a liar's, adding another layer of deceit
to your act, but here I impose family folklore,
which must be packed neat as a suitcase.

In stories, you're the necessary villain,
Elfriede.  So forgive me, if it was nervous
laughter upon realizing, your husband, a Jew,

could be sent back to Europe, to the camps
where the rest of his family had died. Forgive
me, I have to piece together, make conjectures—

we don't know if your name was "Elfriede" or "Elfried."

2.
Little witch, little witch: they'd have me
believe you once crushed men's bones between
the pearls of your teeth, completed the sacrament

with wine, vintage contingent upon the man.
As for grandfather, folklore would offer two
possible storylines: that you laughed, asked him

in how many languages he could call himself
a cuckold, or alternately, that you swallowed
your meal respectfully, knowing he let himself

be devoured.  Little witch, I can't ask you anything
that matters, not now that you are waiting for death
to crush you between his mandibles. Once, you hid

what you were beneath a Greta Garbo hat,
tilted like your smile, arched eyebrows.  I'd guess
your eyes were green. The photo: black and white.

Yes, let's make those eyes emerald, Technicolor.

3.
And then, you emerged in Santiago,
accusing your daughters of abandonment,
virulent in rage, ever an actress

when it was you who vanished, never
to raise them.  The smile of MGM
royalty has disappeared, to be replaced

with, what most closely approximates,
a grimace, though I think you might
consider it a smile.  Again, all I can do

is invent.  Mother goes back and forth
about going to visit; I see her wince
at your current photographs: wizened

stick, almost-man, where once you were
a woman whose curves approximated
a screen siren's: voluptuous in lips,

brow bone, cheeks.  In a recent photo,
you are ecstatic, celebrating your birthday
in a hospital gown, celebrating Christmas,

actually, but my aunt insists it makes
you happy to think that every holiday
belongs to you in this way.  Selfish,

yes.  God knows what else, now that
you're being erased day by day, and yet
if your life were to hold half the secrets

it could hold, anyone might wish instead
to transform into this tiny man who calls
my aunt by my mother's name on Mondays

and by Sunday won't say anything at all.

## Oberwolfach, a Love Poem

*Green, the color of science. Of Germany.*
Frida Kahlo wrote this in a diary entry
where she discussed what colors mean.
In the mathematicians' colony of Oberwolfach,
you are a monk in the forest, working towards
something you can't see: figures and symbols
recalcitrant. Willful. What you want
is to create something new. Or, if not new,
what you might call *an interesting result.*
Frida's art was an interesting result: impaled
by a beam as a young woman, then willingly
subjected to love's mutilations. Together,
husband, we saw "The Two Fridas": one heart
in cross-section, vein leading to a clamp:
two pools of blood so small they resemble
the rosettes at the hem of her white dress,
except one spills into the other. A waterfall.
And the other Frida, holding her hand, wears
Indian clothes. There is another portrait of Frida
as a buck, arrows piercing her sides. A forest,
like the one where thought transports you
farther away than anyone could track.
The sea behind Frida's likeness looks more
like sky than water. Behind and around you,
husband—I want to be the negative space
that a careful hand would trace to make you
visible. I'd like my body to be invisible,
that free of me, that empty.

White

The word for white, that color skin
Comes from "luminous."  White sits
Like a porcelain figure from Castille,
Wearing its lace gloves or white shines
Like an insistent pulse, nuclear flash
Or the blank page of moonlight.

I have never shone, instead my skin
Has taken in the sun like a lover.
Where I come from, marriage
Or money, or both, "can whiten"
And the woman I call mother
Is white, not ivory, her skin
Paper aged by sunlight.

Colonial parchments tell us
Of an Indian woman who ground
Roots of guao and rubbed them
In her hands until she had a fine
Paste to apply to her face, acid
That worked her skin into lace

As she stood before her former
Master and said to him,
*Do you see me now?*
He tried escape, to mock her
While she pursued him
In the huge, outdoor market
While slaves and free men
Watched.  Fanning her words

Into white coals, scalding her
Tongue, she repeated her one
Question.

White was never more white
Than when her mirror face
Reflected his back to him,
Thrice luminous, as terrible
As the moon.
I tell you this
Because few stories can
Approximate what it means

When my father, dark-skinned
Mestizo, screams *stupid,*
*Dirty Indians* at children
Who cross the street
So suddenly he almost
Runs over them.

## Technicolor Sonnet

In her absence, we choose to speak of this:
another husband, another suitor,
to want the banquet and not half-portions—
In her best black and white photograph
and I say best because it's the one she left
behind on purpose, in this curated
keepsake, my grandmother looks like Carole
Lombard, not like Hayworth, not like Garbo,
and so all I ask is that her eyes be green,
an intense Technicolor green, since she was,
above all, an actress, a woman who walked
through Chilean immigration with pounds
of gold jewelry and laughed it off as fake,
a woman who walked away. *Finis.*

When Yellow Beckons

Shade #43 is when I seem more lime-green than chartreuse,
the scent of rain as it seeps into the soil. #37267 is how I drench
canvas in those paint-by-number mini-mall experiences
sought by women who've forgotten dandelion laughter; they might
know shade #5 is the real color of knives even though the other
colors are so self-absorbed. *We make light! We make films together!*
*Look at us, look at us, look at us—red, green, blue.* Whatever.
I am pus, I am sun, I am the bitterness under the tongue
upon awakening. Buttercup, what you call the afterlife
will not be technicolor splendor. Might as well start memorizing
what those other colors look like. I will swallow you yellow.

## Technicolor Sonnet

*Finis.* To be a woman who walks away,
not circumscribed by any narrative,
not the coquette, not the madwoman,
not the woman who made a cuckold
out of my grandfather in 8 different
languages, not my grandmother who died
unsure of her own name, unable to tell
one daughter from another, one country
from the next. Perhaps she might as well
have died alone since everyone became
someone else, musical chairs, pronouns blurred,
mind ambling way from its leash, untethered,
unfettered by love or desire or grief.
*Fin.* Boarding a plane. A woman. *Finis.*

A Glossary of Colors

Nothing is black, really
except for a turkey vulture
as it separates flesh
from a glossy brown pelt
& the wind when it gives
the world its outlines,
the shoulder blade
of reality snapped
back into its socket,
countless wings beating
without ceasing
while the center
of each bird holds
steady, one murmuration
breaking & coming
back together,
breaking & coming
back together
as is right.

Advice My Mother Gave Me about Looking for Rainbows


*after Natalie Kalmus*

That sudden rainfall mixed with sunlight
        might yield just a fraction of rainbow, faded
                watercolor, not Technicolor drenched,

the sky bleeding scarlet or the tiny Emerald
        City beckoning righteous green, not to be confused
                with the copper paint on the witch's face,

flammable poison that indeed ignited, melted
        yielding third-degree burns that howled
                both *what a world what a world* and *my beautiful*

*wickedness* as she died at the feet of a girl
        with red shoes and pigtails and a pill problem
                and the woman who decided all the colors of Oz

decided she should be called *Ringmaster of the Rainbow*
        in her obituary, which seemed sad at first—
                that all of this should be so yields to the initial thought:

that I might be gifted a rainbow should there be water,
        should there be light.

# Technicolor Sonnet

*Finis.* The woman has boarded the plane,
while the man she's abandoned walks away
with a scoundrel, side-by side, confidantes;
my favorite friend is distance, miles
and time zones and my favorite ending
is the shot of the car, blazing ahead
towards the vanishing point, life clarified,
whittled down to what fits in a suitcase,
as if the car could pierce through the screen
of the sky and horizon, as if motion
would mean absolution, erasure
from one storyline so as to begin
in the next.  In this story, I'm color,
saturated emerald, a mallard's neck

# Creation Myth

*For David*

After you turn its key,
one, two, three times
a toy cat creaks
from side to side,
steps forward until blocked,
topples head-first into an
aquarium (fish long gone, only
water & limestone rock).

Down a copper gutter
the stream transforms
into a pond, drop by drop—
until the water is able
to lift a toy soldier
whose foot can now reach
just high enough
to click a fan's switch,
whose wind propels
a roller skate to kick a pail
that topples its release
of one, just one

yellow marble
into a teaspoon catapult
that launches a candy doll
into the air—midair, breath, pause—
should the contraption
work, should the doll fall
into your glass & fizzle,
should you choose to drink
neurons will begin

their pyrotechnic
blue-red-green sizzle
until lips taste salt,
traces of hot cinnamon
& then, a falling backwards—
shoulders missing,
just grazing
the sharp edges
between stars.

# One Drop, Revisited



*"Really, nothing is ever really black"*
          *—Frida Kahlo, diary entry about colors*

*"I black."*
          *—My son, June 12, 2018*

Green was supposed to be the color of science
& Germany. That one I remember quite clearly.
And the fact that Frida didn't believe in black
& common associations with red and blood.
My son is black. He tells me. When he sees
A young man behind the counter at the deli,
He says "dad" because the young man is black
& when we walk around an H&M, he incorporates
Into a family of Haitians or Senegalese or diaspora
French (they are speaking French) because they are
Black and he is black. He knows he's black; bristles
At a white person touching his hair, listens to me
Say "Black is beautiful" when we get to "black,"
Last of the baseball colors—and does not listen
To me—brown skinned, neither here nor there—
Woman whom whites are desperate to excuse
Or invite to sit at the very edge of the table.
What will it cost him, his blackness?
My son somehow knows that it belongs to him,
Either way and at night I hold him against me,
As if I had any power to stop what is to come.

## Protection Spell

My son is the Grand Canyon—
striated gold, browns, vertigo

like the ocean & larger, like dappled azure,
ultramarine inside you until you are floating above

reaching across the chasm to a vision
of a boy, forever at this age—gap-toothed

& copper-perfect, coiled hair growing redder
in the sun while voices declare him *beautiful,*

*such beautiful hair* & we reply, *it's natural,*
which is to say the boy is sacred, inviolable—

a temple inside a temple inside a temple inside
my body, inside my blood, inside each & every cell.

Which is to say I am the mother of a Black boy,
America. Look upon his beauty & bow.

Technicolor Sonnet

To be the emerald of a mallard's neck,
to be redder than the idea of red,
Technicolor drenched, to be rice steeped
in saffron threads, to be shoveled into
a mouth greedy for color, masticated,
swallowed, to become nothing, no, rather,
to be blank, blank as snow, to be canvas
stretched from wall to wall, to have images
projected onto me, become the jilted
suitor in *When Ladies Meet*, the suitor
who proclaims, *I want to be the cream
in her coffee, not the dust beneath her feet*,
to be exactly what she wants and needs.
Just to be longing. That would be it.

ACKNOWLEDGMENTS

Grateful acknowledgment is made to the editors of the following journals and anthologies in which these poems first appeared, sometimes with a different title:

*Apalachee Review*: "My Mother claims that we are related to Hedy Lamarr," "Rin Tin Tin dies in my mother's, not Jean Harlow's, arms"

*Bayou Magazine*: "Technicolor Sonnet (In her absence, we choose to speak of this)"(published as "Finis")

*Bellingham Review*: "Girl as the Color Feral," (published as "Panamanian Diary"); "Prayer" (published as "The Iconography of Small Houses")

*The Canary*: "Portrait of Girls as Technicolor," "Creation Myth." (Canarium Books, 2021)

*Cimarron Review*: "Simultaneous Translation"

*Glass: A Journal of Poetry*: "Ekphrastic Towards a Family"

*Harpur Palate*: "The Ballad of the Quito Tenis"

*Honey Literary Review*: "Slut"

*Portland Review*: "Technicolor Sonnet (To rearrange the actors again and want)" (published as "Silent Movie")

*RHINO*: "To be Rita Hayworthed, First Variation"

*The Shore*: "Oberwolfach, a love poem" and "Technicolor Sonnet (To be the emerald of a mallard's neck)"

*South Carolina Review*: "Bodies of Proof" (published as "Postcards from places I have never been")

*Sugar House Review*: "Technicolor Sonnet (Just to be longing, belong to it)"

I'd like to begin by thanking Chryss Yost and David Starkey of Gunpowder Press for giving *Color Advisory Board* an opportunity to exist in the world; what started off as a crown of sonnets more than a decade ago became a whole book.

I would like to thank my writing teachers: Ha Jin, Peter Ho Davies, Pimone Triplett, and Garrett Hongo. You pushed me to hold myself to a higher standard, and it did make all the difference. I remember what you tried to teach me all those years ago.

I will always be eternally grateful to Lindsay Lusby for guidance at critical stages. She is an amazing poet friend with infallible instincts. For encouragement, especially at the beginning of this project, I'd like to thank Jehanne Dubrow and Jillian Weise, whose friendship and poetic expertise helped me believe in the project. I would also like to thank Anthony Robinson for supporting me as a friend and as a writer throughout this time. More generally, I want to be sure to thank my classmates from the University of Oregon's Creative Writing Program, particularly Major Jackson, Gina Rae Foster, Sonya Posmentier, and Marie Carvalho. They were always careful readers of my poems.

I would also like to thank the Margaret Herrick Library at the Academy of Motion Picture Arts and Sciences which provided access to the Natalie Kalmus papers, and to the librarians there who assisted me in using the materials.

Finally, I'd like to thank my family: Grayson, David, and Chiquita, our dog. You are my sources of love, joy, and healing. My world is full of color because of you. This book would not exist without your formidable support.

# About the Poet

**Michele Santamaría** received her MFA in poetry from University of Oregon, her MLitt in anthropology from University of St. Andrews, Scotland, and her MS in Library Science from Long Island University. Michele's poems are informed by these diverse fields of study and by her experiences living in and between the Americas. Michele's poems have appeared or will appear in *Rhino, Harpur Palate, The Shore, The Canary, Bellingham Review*, and *Cimarron Review*, among others. She received a scholarship from the Breadloaf Writer's Conference, served as a poetry reader for Clemson University's *South Carolina Review*, and served as a senior poetry reader for Washington College's *Cherry Tree*. Michele has also taught poetry to all age groups. As a poet-librarian, Michele published a chapter about poet-librarianship in Poet-Librarians in the Library of Babel and co-wrote a book about teaching research through social media engagement. She lives with her family in Lancaster, Pennsylvania and works at Millersville University as the Learning Design & Student Engagement Librarian, prioritizing the role of wonder in students' research process. Her website is www.michelesantamaria.com.

## Barry Spacks Prize Winners

## DRYDEN-VREELAND BOOK PRIZE
Open to poets working in K-12 education

*Lung Hours*
by Jessica Purdy

*Night Halves*
by Christine Marshall

*Three-Day Weekend*
poems by Christopher Blackman

—

## ALTA CALIFORNIA CHAPBOOKS
*Emma Trelles, Series Editor*
Published in bilingual editions in partnership with **Letras Latinas**,
the literary initiative of the Institute for Latino Studies at
University of Notre Dame

*Patrilineation* by Carlos Andrés Gómez

*Here, on this 76L* by Michelle Moncayo

*Alba and Other Songs* by Fred Arroyo

*The First Amelia* by Amelia Rodriguez

*On Display* by Gabriel Ibarra

*Sor Juana* by Florencia Milito

*Levitations* by Nicholas Reiner

*Grief Logic* by Crystal AC Salas